Church of the Puritans

The Church of the Puritans, Presbyterian : 130th Street, near 5th Avenue New-York

Church of the Puritans

The Church of the Puritans, Presbyterian : 130th Street, near 5th Avenue New-York

ISBN/EAN: 9783337261139

Printed in Europe, USA, Canada, Australia, Japan

Cover: Foto ©Lupo / pixelio.de

More available books at **www.hansebooks.com**

THE
CHURCH OF THE PURITANS

PRESBYTERIAN

130TH STREET, NEAR 5TH AVENUE

NEW-YORK

MDCCCLXXXIX

PREFACE.

This group of sketches is somewhat unusual in form, since it is intended to bear the salutation of a very grateful church to its many friends. It is right that they should know all the detail of labors which they made possible. Such a story may be safely trusted to a charity which has shown itself so wise, so patient and so delicate in earlier days.

There are many who will here find a priceless part of their own history. All infelicities of material and treatment in these pages will be overlooked as they read between the lines. They will gladly review these ⋯ ⋯ past, and say with gratitude: "Thou ⋯ lot. The lines are fallen unto me in ⋯ Yea, I have a goodly heritage."

⋯ in gathering material for the next story, have a special interest in under- ⋯ what has been intrusted to their care.

They will find new reason to respect and love a work whose smallest services have been accomplished with thoughtfulness and sacrifice.

It may be that some who are building for God in other places through much tribulation, will light anew the torch of devotion at the fires which glow, however feebly, in these embers of the past.

CONTENTS.

	PAGE
HISTORICAL	1
BUILDINGS	17
ADMINISTRATION	39
OFFICERS	41
BENEVOLENCES	49
APPOINTMENTS	53
MEMBERSHIP	59
ORIGINAL MEMBERS	64
RECEIVED AND REMOVED	66
PRESENT OR ACCOUNTED FOR	73

LIST OF ILLUSTRATIONS.

The Church Edifice	Frontispiece
Aisle Cornice, East Aisle	3
Corner of Gallery	13
Oak Capital	16
Panel in Gallery Front	19
Screen under Gallery	23
Font — In Memoriam	26
Arcade above Gallery	28
Triple Window in East Transept	30
Iron Cross — East Aisle Window	31
Chancel in the Chapel	34
Book-case in the Chapel	36
Corbels at intersection of Nave and Transept	38

Aisle Cornice — West Aisle 41

The Church as it was dedicated, 1875 44

The Church Interior, enlarged, 1886 50

Stairs to Gallery 51

Interior, from the West Gallery 56

Carved Boss — West Transept Window 58

Aisle Cornice next to West Transept 61

The Chancel 63

Second Corbel from East Transept 65

Boss in Chancel — I. H. S 88

Historical.

> O Sacred Providence who from end to end
>   Strongly and sweetly movest: shall I write
> And not of thee, through whom my fingers bend
>   To hold my quill? Shall they not do thee right?
>
> GEORGE HERBERT: *The Church.*

Preserver of preservers!
Maker of the pure!
Lord of the revolutions of time,
Accomplishment of desires!
All pure things are moved by affection toward Thee;
Pure souls repose their hope in Thee!

PERSIAN LITANY.

IN the summer of 1869 a few earnest souls met in a house on the corner of Lexington Avenue and 128th Street. They were "agreed together" that the tide of population setting toward this part of the city required some new "*labor of love . showed toward his name.*" With this service of prayer the life of the church began.

After many discouragements, consultations, and delays regular public worship commenced in Harlem Hall, November 5, 1871. This hall stands on 125th Street, between Fourth and Lexington Avenues. It seated six hundred. Forty people were gathered for the Sabbath congregations. They had no formal organization, name, property, or pastor. The enterprise was rich in faith.

Early in the following year Rev. Thomas S. Hastings, D. D., writing, as Chairman of the Church Extension Committee of New York, to "P. A. Anner and others associated with him," said: "It is our unanimous opinion that another church should be organized in Harlem."

In accordance with this decision, on the 5th of March, 1872, the presbytery sent its moderator, Rev. C. S. Robinson, D. D., and a committee to recognize "The Second Presbyterian Church of Harlem." We learn from the records that more than half of the original members were not connected with any organization in this part of the city.

The first Sacrament of the Lord's Supper was administered by Rev. J. H. Dwight. His genial, thoughtful, and devout spirit quickened like the sunshine of spring the early life of this enterprise.

The first call was sent to the present pastor, and accepted, July, 1872. He began his labors in September with seventeen families in the parish and twenty-nine scholars in the Sabbath-school.

During the summer four lots had been purchased on West 130th Street, near Fifth Avenue, for $36,000. The first thousand dollars which secured the purchase came from one whose aid has been foremost in every work. There were in addition $17,000 subscribed by the parish, with the agreement that it should be returned in pew value when the church should be completed.

The installation of the pastor took place Oct. 24th. Rev. John Hall, D. D., preached the sermon. Prayer was offered by Rev. Robert Booth, D. D. The charge to the pastor was given by Rev. Howard

Crosby, D. D., and to the people by Rev. J. O. Murray, D. D. An address was made by Rev. Thomas S. Hastings, D. D.

In December the Church Extension Committee promised $10,000 in aid of a new building. The parish withdrew all claims upon their former subscriptions and added still larger gifts. Many promises of assistance were made to the pastor. Rev. George B. Cheever, D. D., offered the church the funds resulting from the sale of the lease of the Church of the Puritans in Union Square. The value of this property, which had been invested largely in lots, Dr. Cheever estimated to be $87,000. Three conditions accompanied this gift. Two were later withdrawn by Dr. Cheever. The third was gladly observed in perpetuating the name of "The Church of the Puritans."

In early April the city courts gave notice that in a week they should occupy Harlem Hall. Six days later a wooden chapel was planned, built, furnished, and occupied on the vacant grounds opposite the present buildings.

This tabernacle was, however, unsuitable to cold weather. The necessity for a permanent edifice was evident. The friend who led the way in obtaining the lots, gave the first thousand dollars for laying the foundations of the building. Contractors were found who dug the cellar without cost and gave nearly a thousand dollars for the earth removed, besides leaving the best of the building sand behind.

At this time services in the work of constructing the building were freely offered by the members of the church. The names only of those who have passed into the "temple not made with hands" may properly be mentioned here.

L. C. Dye, a builder by trade, gave his large experience in superintending the masons. Alexander Maxwell, hearing that the estimates for stone were discouraging, undertook that part of the building with a saving of $30,000. He gave much of the ornamental work and provided the rest at cost. His aid was also felt in every part of the undertaking. The church is his monument. To the care of these two men is due the perfect condition of the masonry after sixteen years. George Hill made the decoration possible, and left the reflection of his own delicate and devout soul upon the walls. Henry C. Bayne wrought with marvelous skill and economy in framing and furnishing, refusing all recompense for superintending. He was satisfied if by his labor he might serve acceptably the "Carpenter of Nazareth." After sixteen years of incessant care for the house of God, Henry Bayne has entered into rest, leaving his faithful and modest work among the most honored traditions of the place. P. A. Anner and George Moores gave the window frames. The burdens of building material, plumbing, and transportation were greatly lightened by those who are still with us.

Special gifts followed. Among these were the communion furniture, eleven richly decorated windows, the sedilia in the church and chapel, the pulpit, books, tables, the chancel and chapel carpets,— the bronze hinges of the doors, the font, and the offering plates. Even the organ itself, which has added so much to the comfort of troubled souls, and to the inspiration of worship through these many years, was, with its case, a gift. There were also offered manual labor, legal services, and financial credit in times of greatest need. The music fell into kindly hands. One voice will be especially associated with unwavering faith and warmest friendship. Another voice, which elsewhere had been highly rewarded, was given gladly here through five years of uninterrupted service. These many labors were alike builded into the church and were above all price.

The trustees did not have to consider any expenses except for ordinary material. They also knew that a great reserve of financial strength had not yet been called upon. A buyer was ready to take the real estate as soon as an enablement act should have passed the legislature. In this property also waited reënforcements. When, therefore, the 26th day of June, 1873, the corner-stone was laid, the prospects of the church were as fair as the day itself.

Rev. George B. Cheever, D. D., made the address in his peculiarly impressive and graceful way. Rev. M. R. Vincent, D. D., Rev. Charles S. Robinson, D. D., and Rev. Howard Crosby, D. D., gave expression to the most generous sympathy of the presbytery.

The sealed box which once rested in the corner-stone at Union Square was placed beside a new box which contained "the short and simple annals of" this church. There were also two volumes by Dr. Cheever and an address to those who should open the box by that much loved man Rev. C. J. Warren, who with two others were the only church members who brought their letters from Union Square to 130th Street.

On that afternoon, when the corner-stone was laid, the congregation went out from the shadow which lengthened from the western wall, with undisturbed faith that they would dedicate the church soon, and that too without debt.

The financial panic came suddenly. Not a family escaped. Fortunes disappeared. Subscriptions failed. The lots given by the Church of the Puritans, and temporarily mortgaged, were foreclosed. A loss from the original estimates of $48,000 in this property alone was realized. The church building was abandoned.

Winter storms sifted through the bare rafters. The chapel was finished with serious joy.

Notwithstanding all discouragements, the congregation outgrew the chapel before Spring came. The friends of the parish and, most of all, the creditors, urged the completion of the church in view of the larger income.

Then the people settled down with wonderful cheerfulness to bear new burdens. Luxuries and pleasures alike were laid aside. There were many acts of heroic self-denial. No one thought of seeking assistance or expected that it would ever be needed. It did not seem possible that the business depression could last much longer. These two years of self-sacrifice made Christian character fast.

The church was dedicated April 15, 1875, with a funded debt of $60,000 and a floating debt of $20,000. In the sermon of Rev. George B. Cheever, D. D., the prayer of Rev. Philip Schaff, D. D., and the addresses of Rev. Dr. Hall, Dr. Booth, Dr. Conkling, Dr. White, and Dr. Robinson there was a tone of perfect confidence in the ultimate prosperity of the church. The debt was indeed increasing, but so also was the parish. It was a question of holding on and wishing for the day.

But the financial storm also held on. The most heroic efforts must have their limit. In the spring of

1878 the end was reached. Foreclosure proceedings were commenced.

The Church Extension Committee, the most wise and kind of friends, with the help of the estate of John C. Greene, proposed to pay the funded debt if the parish would take care of all other obligations.

The people, so long and heavily burdened, could not give at once $45,000 more. Two patient and wise trustees asked each creditor what, under the circumstances, they wished. Some freely relinquished a third of their claim, some more, some less. The amount needed to satisfy all creditors was $13,000. If this could be raised at once the church would be free of debt. Otherwise the efforts of another church, well under way, would result in taking the property forever from the parish. This announcement was made on Sabbath day and a week was given for serious thought.

The beauty of the following May Sabbath added a new feeling of hope. The morning service was burdened with suspense. At its close all were invited to the chapel. The benediction was followed by a moment of perfect stillness. Then the entire congregation silently entered the adjoining room.

One of the trustees, upon whose interview with the creditors the life of the church depended, presided at this meeting with a quiet, intense interest. His perfect calmness was shared by all. The trustee who had been associated with him waited to record the offerings. A statement was made that no sum would be used unless the entire amount, $13,000, could be raised. Yet the first gift was a check for $500, so great was the faith of one who said: "I may end in want, but the church must not." A child's gift of one dollar followed. Then quickly with suppressed tears and beating hearts, offerings were made as the result of so much thought and prayer that not one gift failed to be made good afterward. There were pledges for children and children's children. One large contribution came by telegraph from abroad. One from precious friends of earlier days who came to help the work that morning. Every one took part as they could.

The experience of that hour cannot be recorded. It cannot be repeated. It cannot be forgotten. The darkness broke. But many men went out from the place like Jacob from Peniel, princes at heart, to carry forever the marks of the struggle.

One large-hearted man, then a stranger, but since a trusted officer of the church, came at noon with a great gift. Others heard the story and eagerly took part in the work.

The Sabbath-school had but commenced its exercises in the afternoon when a little girl brought, in a wooden pail, all her possessions, to the superintendent's table. By a spontaneous movement the school came crowding forward and heaped in little coin $800 upon the table. And thus, by over four hundred separate offerings, the debt ended with the day.

The debt was paid. But fearing lest a property so hardly saved should in the future be endangered by another mortgage, and desiring to make forever sure to the denomination the money provided by the Church Extension Committee, a mortgage was given, without interest, to the Presbytery of New York. It was not intended that this should ever be repaid. But in many living streams of benevolence the clouds of mercy which came up upon the church that day are now flowing back again.

The debt was paid, yet not a few creditors have had occasion to know that the church recognizes obligations not provided for by law. Doubtless hereafter others will see to it that the precept "owe no man anything," shall have its widest interpretation in the history of this parish.

The debt was paid and the impulse was felt in the deeper current of Christian life. From these financial barriers, like mountain streams, the influence of the church went quietly on its widening way.

It would not be possible, and it might not be best for a people trained to independent thought, to escape difference of opinion. But every difficulty has served in the interest of a still more united and prosperous work for Christ. It is a matter of grateful remembrance that through all festivals which circumstances have made necessary not a single disagreement has disturbed the harmony of the work.

In the year 1883, an Easter offering replaced the wooden fence with the present granite coping and iron rail. A new stairway and fire escapes were added to the chapel.

Corner of Gallery

Three years later, as more room was required, the galleries were built at a cost of $8000. Other improvements were made at the same time. The spirit of special giving, which had enriched the church so often and blessed those who took part in it, added the memorial window of the west transept, the pastor's chair, the flower table, sedilia, choir screen, the drapery of the screen and doorways, the stairs on either side the pulpit, and the rich panels in the center of the gallery bays. Again a kind, helpful hand was seen in the new organ case, and in the moving of the organ from the west transept. It is a peculiar delight in such memorials to mingle our deepest experiences with the service of God. Troubled and weary as well as happy souls, in the association of their individual lives with the kingdom of the common Master, anticipate the perfect worship beyond.

From the earliest days the benevolences of the church have been regular and systematic. No pressure at home has interrupted work for those who are without. A mission school has been supported at Manhattanville, or on Second Avenue. The record of 1884 may serve as an example. In that year the Woman's Society spent $812 in providing work and relief for the poor. The Cemah Club used $1250 in assisting 210 families. The deacons' fund reported a balance of $400 in the treasury. The Sabbath-school, in an average attendance of 288, added to the church offering $600 for missionary purposes, all but nine taking part in the service. In this year also a very busy people spent 13,200 hours as followers of Him "who went about doing good."

As each year has increased the church and parish, so in the matter of benevolence every season yields more fruit than the one from which its life sets forth. The aggregate of giving in this brief history, by small sums, with self-denial, and without special effort save on one great day, amounts, for its own and for missionary use, to a sum exceeding $400,000.

It need not be added that in the decoration of this building, as of the tabernacle of old, which they spoke of as a living thing, the one thought kept carefully in mind is the service of Him who is the sacrifice for us all. It is the spirit which gladly broke the alabaster box. Some may wonder "wherefore this waste," but many more, in unconscious preparation for the solemn events which overtake us all, will rejoice in the opportunity to please that Master, and will be glad that this story of a devout church should go some little distance "throughout the whole world" in honor of His name.

"God is not unrighteous to forget your work and labor of love which ye have showed toward His name — in that ye have ministered to the saints and do minister . show the same diligence . unto the end . for God made promise . blessing, I will bless thee, and multiplying, I will multiply thee."

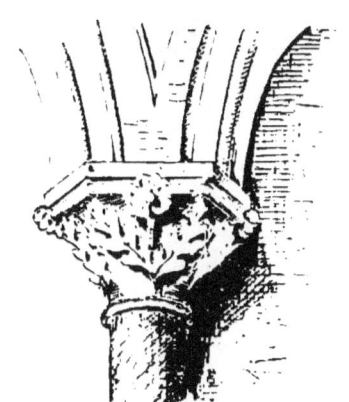

Buildings.

Walk about Zion, and go round about her; tell the towers thereof. Mark ye well her bulwarks, consider her palaces: that ye may tell it to the generation following. For this God is our God for ever and ever: he will be our guide even unto death.
Psalm xlviii.

Building is a sweet impoverishing.
Spanish Proverb.

    If thou chance for to find
    A new house to thy mind,
    And built without thy cost:
      Be good to the poor
      As God gives thee store,
    And then my labour 's not lost.
Inscription on church building: Bemerton, 16

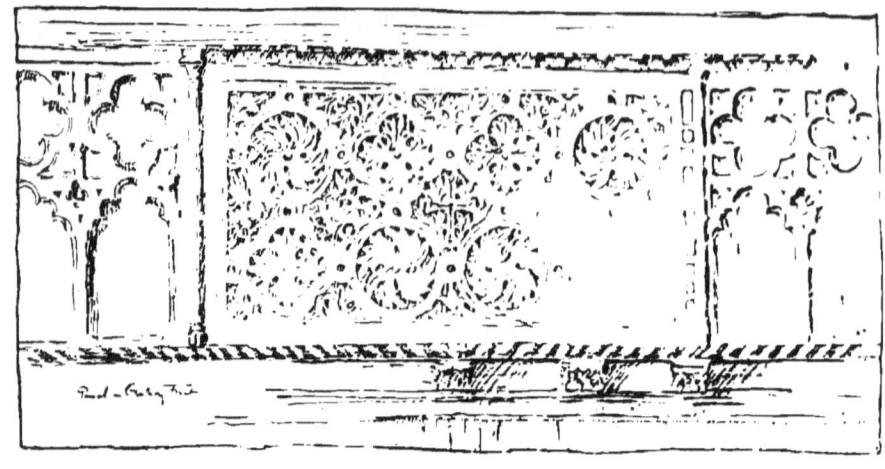

IN answer to the question, How should a church be built? the reply was made long ago: "So as to give glory to God and exalt men's souls to sanctity." The psalmist is able to "give unto the Lord glory due his name," because he comes with an offering into noble courts, where "Honor and majesty are before Him. Strength and beauty are in his sanctuary." The royal builder also refused to "offer unto the Lord my God of that which doth cost me nothing." It comes to pass in all times that a meeting place with God, when it represents an earnest spirit, advances from the convenience of a shelter from the weather into the form of an offering, and the word of God is richer and more impressive because wood and stone are "silent voices which speak for God and his salvation."

The early English style of architecture was chosen for these buildings because it expresses a spirit of devotion, and therefore becomes helpful in worship. In a sparing use of cut stone, in the strong rubble work of the walls, in firm yet graceful arches, in deep hollows and bold rounds, as well as in the honesty of purpose shown in the use of uniting string courses, windows which let in light, buttresses which support, piers which sustain, and cornices which bind together, it confirms the saying of Coleridge: "A Gothic church is Christianity cut in stone."

To this end—the glory of God and the worship of men—worked the architect James W. Pirsson. And the people worked with him, gladly led by his brilliant, devout, and kindly spirit, and esteeming him highly for his work's sake.

A neighboring quarry furnished the white marble. It was treated in broken ashlar, because in that form innumerable shadows soften the glare of the sun, and because it affords contrast with the carved work. Like all stone in its native climate it stands well. By reason of easy transportation it served also the demands of economy.

In the center of the main building are three porches. Beneath these are the three large doors recessed with slender columns. Above the doors rise three pointed gables. The tympanum of each arch carries the symbol of eternity. On the spring of these arches are plainly cut three words, reading from left to right: "No man cometh to the Father but by me." "God is our refuge and strength." "He dwelleth with you and shall be in you." Those who enter and he who runs may read in these texts our declaration of faith in the Trinity. The foliated capitals set in the walls from which the outer arches spring, and also the capitals of the two columns of dark polished granite which stand as firmly as Jachin and Boaz in the center, carry the spirit of the words. The saying of Christ rises from "lilies among thorns," and ends in the "passion flower and olive." The central word about the Father rises from the thought of " rest in strife"—the olive amid passion flowers—and is complete in the grapes and wheat. The promise of the Holy Spirit commencing in the suggestion of strength at the communion, "the vine and wheat," is completed in the capital which bears triumphal palms.

Beneath the central valleys of these gables are carved on the left a spray of vine and on the right a branch of sturdy oak.

The stone finials which surmount these porches and complete the main gable above them are cut into the conventional clover leaf of the thirteenth century. These leaves were associated with piety and safety, because they seemed to fold themselves together in prayer and trust as the sun went down.

Within the main gable is a marigold window, resting upon a deep sill and surrounded by rich moldings, which in turn are supported by granite columns. The light through this window throws the shadow of a cross by day upon the congregation and by night upon the street.

On the left, the heavy moldings of the gable die away into a tower which has a wedge-shaped roof. The two lower stories of this tower serve for vestibules and stairways to the gallery and to the room above. The third floor was intended for a pastor's study. Here the main window is divided by a mullion. It represents in the glass on one side a lamp with the motto for the indoor work, "Thy word is a lamp to my feet," and on the other side a shepherd's crook and a crown with reference to service abroad, "When the chief shepherd shall appear he shall give thee a crown of glory."

On the first floor of the tower a door opens into the hall. Across this hall a second door leads to a passageway outside the walls, by which the pastor's room near the pulpit is reached.

On the eastern side of the church the main elevation is broken by a lobby, a single story in height, with deep-set lancet windows. This lobby opens toward the East upon the lawn. With the main vestibule it forms a corridor sixty-five feet long across the entire front of the building.

In the place usually occupied by a wall, an open screen of ash, filled with glass, like the arcade of Beverly minster, separates the vestibule from the audience-room. This figured and colored glass excludes air and sound, while it gives a pleasant welcome, and forms an easy

Screen under Gallery

transition from the confusion and brightness of the street to the quiet of the audience-room.

The floor of the vestibule is laid with tiles in which the mats are sunk. The ceiling is of natural wood. Within the vestibule, where a single wall supports the main building, the main porch, and the lobby, the corner-stone was placed. It seemed friendly to shelter it from the weather. Upon its east and west faces of polished granite are cut inscriptions from the old and new Testament, and between them is the Lord's saying: "Behold I lay in Zion . . . a corner-stone." "Jesus Christ himself being the chief corner-stone." "Upon this rock will I build my church."

The audience-room has the form of a Roman basilica, with the tribune or apse opposite the entrance, and columns dividing the nave from the aisles or "alleys." The clear-story and the roof is broken into a transept, though the side walls beneath are in line with the aisles.

The rear or south wall rises gracefully in three lines of arcades, with a diminishing number of arches, the highest supporting the rose window. The northern wall — the chancel — has a single arch.

An open, timbered roof rests lightly yet firmly upon brackets, spandrils, and hammer beams. The panels of the roof are decorated in light blue or gilt bronze for the purpose of reflecting the light. The arch above the apse rises from four polished granite columns sixty-five feet above the floor. The ceiling is groined and ornamented with heavy bosses. In the center are the letters I.H.S. The spaces between the moldings are treated in deep blue monocrome, with stars.

The apse contains the organ and the choir, which the old service book calls "the place where they do sing." From this elevation, neither far above nor behind the congregation, the singing is most effectively led by the choir. The seat of the minister stands on one side in order that he also may by reason of the distance intelligently join in the worship.

In front of the rich choir screen is a bench of oak with gothic carving, the memorial of a dear child. The massive pastor's chair, a table for books, a flower table which is also a memorial gift, and the pulpit, furnish the chancel.

Above the organ is a rose window having eight openings about the center. In four of these openings are Greek letters arranged like a cross, reminding us of Christ. "The Beginning," "The End," "Divine," "Risen." In the center of all is the descending dove of the Holy Spirit. It was the gift of one of the youngest members of the parish.

Upon the communion platform stand a table and two chairs. The capitals of the shafts upon which "the board" of the table rests are carved into reeds and thorns. The chairs have panels of grapes and wheat. The cornice of the table continually speaks to the worshipers in the words, "Do this in remembrance of me." The giver of this table is also remembered in the west aisle window where the lilies forever bloom. It was her single wish that the table should be finished with equal care on all sides as it was not intended so much to be seen by men as to express "in a small gift a great love for Christ." Scarcely was it finished before she went to meet her Master in the kingdom of God.

The marble font beside the table bears on its eight

Font

panels gothic forms. It is made of the same stone of which the church is built. Above the shaft it is wreathed with lotus leaves and flowers, which were most dear to her with whom it is associated. The words upon the base suggest the use of the font and the spirit of one of the purest, simplest, and most affectionate of God's children: "Of such is the kingdom of heaven."

On either side the pulpit, broad stairways lead to the galleries. They are like the chancel itself carpeted in crimson. They unite the congregation above with those who worship on the main floor. By their warmth of color as well as by their use they lend a friendly air to the apse. They would also be a matter of safety in time of danger.

The offering plates, with carved borders, represent Gothic leaves folded upon one another as if they had caught the spirit of the giver, and wished to hide the gifts they served. These plates fitly rest upon the communion table. The plates and the table are memorials of a similar devotion.

In the organ screen of panel work are two entrances which are hung with deep blue curtains, embroidered with pomegranates, after the manner of the tabernacle. One opening leads into the pastor's room. The other is used by the choir, who enter by the chapel.

It is a most pleasant thought that in this apse, or chancel,—as it is called from cancellus, a screen,—everything was provided by the care of some kindly heart. The sacred recollections of thirty families are represented here.

Nor do such associations confine themselves to this place. On the west side of the transept is a sedilia, built by one who, though unknown to this people, loved them well. The light of their loyalty to the common Master lighted his path of suffering into the "rest which remains for the people of God."

Above the stairways which rise from the pulpit are figured windows. The group of three windows on

the east are, in their subjects, suggestive of the font below, and the room behind them which was intended for little children. They represent the presentation of Christ in the temple, the baptism of Christ, and Christ among the doctors. The memorial initials are M. G. C., I. H. A., M. L. H. They are the blessed recollection of two mothers and one "man of God."

On the other side of the chancel is the "Tree of life." The day is kindling upon a distant city wall, and upon the hills and fields, but most of all it floods the leaves and fruit of the tree itself. Whatever be the weariness of the sky without, in brilliant tones it teaches the lesson of a young life which ripened into rare thoughtfulness and sweetness under the burden and heat of trial here, and then with a benediction passed into the unfading splendor of the paradise of God. The inscription reads: "Blessed are they that . . . have a right to the tree of life and may enter in through the gates into the city." "In memoriam, J. M. R."

Within the chancel there are two other windows. The west window sets forth the joyful side of worship with figures of pipes and trumpets, "O come, let us sing unto the Lord." On the east, is the pilgrim's staff and wallet, "My grace is sufficient for thee." The latter window opens easily into a room where invalids can join in the service, and not be seen as they come or go. It is reached by the tower door and upper chapel.

Other windows have their special meaning. The rose window in the east transept bears the date of the first Easter in the church, when it was given at the morning offering.

The great west geometric window carries the lesson, "Let not your heart be troubled," E. H. D. In memoriam E. H. D. L., "There remaineth a rest." It was given by J. A. Dudley, who, with untiring devotion, lived and labored for the church until he

Triple window in East Transept

passed into the light where we no more are obliged to "see through a glass darkly."

The aisle window nearest the transept is sacred to the memory of J. H. Dwight, whose mantle of love fell on the church in its early days.

Still south in the same aisle, broken by a mullion, is a window resplendent with palms and lilies. It teaches a lesson of faith: "Consider the lilies." It has also, wrought into the design itself, the song of those who bear palms. A triumphant faith distinguished the life of the accomplished and noble woman who is remembered here. Her courage and her bright spirit were a continual blessing to the church. Her life was a call to service and an example of devotion. Very few have such opportunities of doing good. No one has ever better used them. The window glows as with a memory like that which made holy the burning bush.

In the east aisle window the figures of the Marys and the angels at the tomb bring to mind another saint — S. J. C., "In Pace." "The Lord is Risen, Hallelujah."

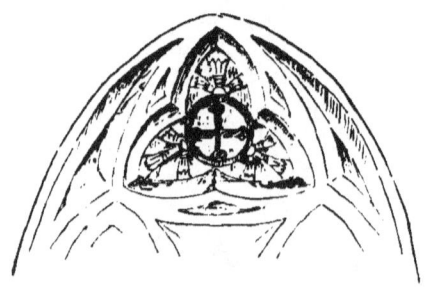

In the apex of this window is the shadow of an iron cross whose meaning she knew so well. It was the greatest treasure she possessed, and may possibly have been seen by St. Mark in Egypt.

When the church was built galleries were provided for in the elevation of the side walls. These aisle galleries have therefore room to pass under the transept arches and beyond. Between the columns which carry the clear-story they project in bays, ornamented with Gothic panels. The use of boxes and chairs gives the effect of great comfort. Every seat commands a view of the chancel.

The clear-story secures a natural and abundant supply of light, all the more pleasing as the congregation faces the north. There cannot from the aisle windows alone be secured a perfect relief from the shadow of the galleries. Artificial light in dark mornings is needful in this part of the church. The three rose windows also lend much light, although they are placed too high to disturb the eyes of the worshiper. Whatever of value belongs to masses of sober and pure color relieved by rich diaper patterns in the soffit of the arches and on the chancel walls is carefully secured. No part of the decoration intrudes itself. Even the tints of the rolled cathedral glass blend with the general effect of the walls, and altogether give an impression of quiet hospitality.

The solid decorations of the audience-room are bosses and brackets, capitals and frieze, numbering over a hundred pieces and weighing many thousand pounds. They are all carved and given by rude but reverent hands, with the mind of early days when men loved to "think God's thoughts after him," in shaping for His house passion flowers and ivy, celery and "lilies of the field."

The ventilation of the building is secured by indirect

supplies of air through five adjoining rooms. The supply of artificial light, for the greater part hidden in the returns of the transepts, and high above the columns, is made to aid the current of air. The burners are lighted in sections by electricity and the escape of gas is thus avoided.

There are ten doors in the main church and eight generous openings into the street.

Not less than a thousand persons can be seated in the audience-room. Yet so harmonious are the proportions, so well balanced are the decorations, so simple and evident are the relations of each part of the building to the rest, no one thinks of any cleverness in the construction or of the dimensions of the place. Everything seems near, convenient, dignified, cheerful. Alike removed from excitement or wonder or love of controversy, the solemn delight of the psalmist pervades the place. " Let us come before his presence with thanksgiving . . . O come, let us worship and bow down; let us kneel before the Lord our Maker."

A large door under the east gallery stairs opens into the lower chapel. A second door in the east gallery leads to the landing by the upper Sabbath-school-room. This door is close by the way which the children throng each Sabbath. It reminds us of the story of a very dear and patient little sufferer who once walked here. It is a memorial door, and on the frame is carved the promise, "He shall carry the lambs in his arms." H. P. L.

From the lawn a deep-set doorway opens into the east vestibule, which shares with the stairway the lower story of the main tower. The capitals of the four granite columns which stand by the entrance represent the foliage of the four quarters of the Holy Land—oak, pomegranate, thorn, and almond.

The lower story of the chapel is lighted from the

street by three windows, whose moldings relieve the outer wall by strong shadows. The wall of the second story retreats and breaks into the roof by a small dormer window resting on dwarf columns.

From the vestibule of the east tower two doors open into the lower chapel. This room seats about three hundred and fifty. Here for many months the church worshiped, oppressed with the burden of debt, yet realizing by the trouble their strength of endurance. Its chancel has therefore many sacred associations.

As this room was intended for evening service, it is only lighted at either end by seven windows. It serves also for the meetings of the Guild and for the smaller children of the Sabbath-school. The ash case in this room is a memorial of that rare worker Mrs. E. H. D. Lyon, and is used for missionary work, to which her life was devoted.

The upper chapel is abundantly lighted on the north side by six windows, each twelve feet high. There are four windows on the south side, and a large skylight in the center of the open timbered roof. The subjects of the south windows belong to the Sabbath-school. On one side Eli is teaching Samuel, and beside them the good shepherd carries the lamb. In the center window Mary teaches our Lord. In the right window Timothy is taught by his mother, and the other half of the window represents Christ with children in his arms. The dormer window contains the heads of Cherubs, with a dove.

The open roof, by its height, secures comparative silence and perfect ventilation for the Sabbath-school.

On the south side a large case contains in three sections, the library, a place for water, and a closet. The small room adjoining this upper chapel is used by a Bible class. From this room an iron stairway is reached, by which a safe escape is provided in case of fire in the tower.

In the upper chapel various services and festivals are held. It serves as a church drawing-room. This use

Bookcase in Chapel

of the building has never been a prominent part of church life. In the basement of the church are ample conveniences for closets containing dishes, tables, and chairs. Here also is the range, the gift of a valued friend.

One thing remains incomplete — the spire. It seemed better to wait until it could be finished in stone. The tower is carried above the second group of windows. After eighteen years of incessant giving in things temporal and spiritual that most faithful man, Joseph A. Dudley, made provision in his will to assist in building this spire. His spirit rests in many hearts. The devotion which laid broad foundations and watched with delight the stones rise, "line upon line," above stained glass and sober roof, above the stretch of solid wall and shadow of slender buttress, will not be satisfied until the finial crowns the slender spire nine score feet above the lawn, and all the people joyfully repeat the word: "Unto Thee, O Lord, do I lift up my soul. Lord, I have loved the habitation of thine house, and the place where thine honor dwelleth."

Corbels at intersection of Nave and Transept

Administration.

Thyself and thy belongings
Are not thine own so proper, as to waste
Thyself upon thy virtues, they on thee.
Heaven doth with us as we with torches do;
Not light them for themselves: for if our virtues
Did not go forth of us, 't were all alike
As if we had them not. Spirits are not finely touched
But to find issues.
MEASURE FOR MEASURE.

Good is no good but if it be spend,
God giveth good for none other end.
SPENSER.

Where shall charity be found? In the footprint of one bound on works of charity and faith; in the merciful spirit; in lips that dwell lovingly on that which the great Teacher hath taught us to adore.
SINGHALESE-BUDDHIST.

OFFICERS.

PASTOR.

Rev. EDWARD L. CLARK, D. D.   29 West 130th Street.

RULING ELDERS.

R. T. B. EASTON	223 West 128th Street.
P. S. ELY ...	40 West 126th Street.
F. A. ERWIN	259 West 128th Street.
W. H. PAINE	107 West 122d Street.
T. J. RUSH	700 East 134th Street.
A. S. WALKER	157 West 122d Street.

DEACONS.

J. B. CARSS	17 East 133d Street.
D. S. WENDELL	128 East 128th Street.
FREDERICK E. DICKENSON	286 St. Nicholas Avenue.

SUPERINTENDENT OF SABBATH-SCHOOL.

T. H. BALDWIN   128 West 132d Street.

TRUSTEES.

J. D. PLATT	311 Lenox Avenue.
T. H. BALDWIN	221 West 132d Street.
JAS. H. BEALS, Jr.	36 West 130th Street.
CHARLES W. DAYTON	9 West 128th Street.
J. E. DOW	2290 Seventh Avenue.
J. A. HAMILTON	319 East 124th Street.
WILLIAM C. HOLBROOK	10 West 130th Street.
C. W. WELLS	2203 Sixth Avenue.
W. I. VAN DOLSEN	122 West 130th Street.

MUSICAL DIRECTOR.

ALBERT J. HOLDEN   109 East 103d Street.

The Church of the Puritans belongs to the Presbytery of the city of New York.

A Presbytery is composed of all the ministers and one ruling elder from each church within its bounds. At its regular meetings it considers appeals from sessions, examines, ordains, installs candidates for the Holy Ministry, receives new members, and attends to any other business which concerns the peace or prosperity of so much of the Kingdom of Christ as is entrusted to its care.

A Synod represents a group of Presbyteries. The General Assembly meets once each year. All business sent up from the Presbyteries through the Synods passes in review. This is the highest judicatory of the Presbyterian Church in matters affecting doctrine or discipline.

The Book of Discipline is published by order of the General Assembly as the constitution which regulates these various bodies, including the local sessions.

This book contains The Confession of Faith, the Catechisms, and the Directory for the Worship of God. Its opening declaration, first published in 1788, expresses the "unanimous opinion" of the Presbyterian Church : " God alone is Lord of the conscience, and hath left it free from the doctrines and commandments of men, which are in anything contrary to His word or beside it in matters of faith or worship." "Therefore," continues our present Book of Discipline, "they consider the rights of private judgment in all matters that respect religion as universal and unalienable."

In such a spirit the word discipline is restored to its meaning of discipleship to Him whose word shall make us "free indeed." It would be well to keep also the word *presbyterian* in its scriptural use, and remember that St. Paul urges Timothy to make the largest use of the liberty which comes with the gift of prophecy, but to use it in the order of that church discipline which is suggested by "the laying on of the hands of the presbytery."

ELDERS.

In the Presbyterian Form of Government, Chapter V., it is said, "Ruling elders are properly the representatives of the people, chosen by them for the purpose of exercising government and discipline in connection with pastors or ministers." In usage these officers are often distinguished as Ruling Elders from the minister, who is a Preaching Elder.

The body of elders is known as a Session. They direct religious services, including the Sabbath-school, together with all matters pertaining to the spiritual interests of the parish. They preside also at the annual meeting for business. They distribute the elements on sacramental occasions. They admit members to the church. They keep the records of the church. They are the trusted counsel of the pastor. They are in the labors of the church, "the bond of perfectness." Col. iii, 14.

At present the number of elders is six, serving in three groups for three years. It is understood and desired that the office should be, in fact, perpetual. Yet the system of reëlection gracefully provides for any changes in this office which may seem necessary.

By the Form of Government, Chap. XIII., p. 2, male members in full communion in the church in which they are to exercise their office are eligible to become elders.

All communicants are expected to take part in the election. After a nomination by the session, anyone may present a name for such election.

DEACONS.

THE deacons have the care of the Lord's table, and the sacramental offering for the Lord's poor. The by-laws of the church provide for three deacons, whose election occurs at the same time and manner with the elders. The form of ordination for both offices is similar, and both are required to subscribe to the Westminster Catechism, as embodying the substance of doctrine taught in the scriptures.

The Church as it was dedicated 1875.

THE NEW YORK
PUBLIC LIBRARY

ASTOR LENOX
TILDEN

TRUSTEES.

The trustees are legal representatives of the parish in the collection and disbursement of income and in the care of the buildings. The parish looks to them for lead in all financial movements, and has loyally supported them in every crisis of its history.

Three trustees are elected yearly for a term of three years. Anyone who has contributed to the support of the society according to the usage and custom thereof for one year, if they be of full age, are entitled to vote at such elections.

It would seem from the difficult and often perplexing nature of the work, not less than the fact that it is a "labor of love," that every member of the parish is under special obligation to assist in all such elections and keep himself informed of the work accomplished. Such interest from all who care for the dignity and prosperity of the church is indispensable.

SABBATH-SCHOOL.

Officers of the Sabbath-school are elected subject to the approval of the session.

All expenses of the school are met by the trustees. The offerings are devoted entirely to missionary purposes.

The members of the school are not rewarded for attendance in any way. At Christmas an entertainment expresses the deep regard of the parish for the school, but the presents provided are brought by the children for the poor and sick. Whether the special interest of that evening is a model of the *Mayflower*, fully rigged, manned, and setting sail, or the festivities of an English Christmas-tree, or a Christmas procession, the cargo of the one, the fruit of the second, and the lading of the third consists in gifts for poor children. This form of keeping holidays has commended itself so much to the parish, that at the last festival thirty-seven bushels of "things new and old" were sent about doing good. Evidently the young people keep no small part of the pleasure they give. The word in this way of self-denial for Christ's sake gives proof of its power in the ministry of love.

THE PARISH.

Those who wish to make the church widely and thoroughly useful should remember how dependent the officers are upon them for information of any in the congregation who are sick or needy. They are glad at all times to serve those who may not be in any other parish. Every believer has as truly a call to take part in these various services as the officers themselves. The usefulness of those who lead must be measured by the support of those who follow. This is as necessary now as it was in the day when the apostle wrote to Thessalonians: "Ye became followers of us and of the Lord, having received the word in much affliction with joy in the Holy Ghost—examples to all—to serve the living and true God."

Among the lessons of the past nothing has been more clear than the wisdom of leaving the necessities of the church to the generous and earnest consideration of the people. Because, with scarcely an exception, abundant and constant assistance has come without solicitation, those who could not give have been saved embarrassment, and those who had the means to give have enjoyed the rich blessing of a spontaneous offering. The attitude of the church has always been, "We seek not yours, but you."

There are, however, constant inquiries which always follow successful and happy labors. What more can we do? What is needed to enlarge the usefulness of the church? In what way could my means be wisely invested "in His name"? To these it may be said:

1. A fund would be of great value, which should be held in trust for the care and improvement of the building.

2. It would be a kindly service to endow free pews.

3. The Session have need of an income for continued use in lines of which the regular charities cannot take notice. In the administration of religious affairs such relief would be a perennial blessing.

4. The friendly services of some judicious woman employed by the church would multiply greatly the

light and comfort we are so anxious to extend to the poor and sick.

5. A Puritan House should be hired or bought in some one of the many neglected neighborhoods near us. In such a house the Helping Hand would have a depository of food, medicine, and clothes to give or lend. Here also they would on Thursdays "entertain strangers." On Sabbath the children could be taught the Scriptures, and on week-days useful trades and industries. A day nursery could care for the health and comfort of little people, and thus allow their industrious parents to earn a living, and at the same time the children would be trained for a greater economy and better self-support than otherwise they could obtain in the struggle for life. When the sun goes down, a library, a bright reading room, plain talks, and healthful entertainments might lay hands of healing on many young souls who now roam the streets without help in "divers diseases" of mind and body. What a meeting-house would this become—a Bethel—to wanderers! It would be full of ministering spirits, ascending and descending from homes of comfort and intelligence! What a relief in sorrow would earnest workers find here, as they seek new spheres for the dear toil they have bestowed on souls now with the cloud of witnesses! What a noble memorial of some kindly life would such a cen-

ter of Christian industry remain! "Their works do follow them."

BENEVOLENCES.*

The Puritan Association is composed of all the officers and one delegate from each society in the parish. This council harmonizes appointments and labors, keeps every part of the line informed of whatever aggressive work is undertaken, and insures both sympathy and assistance where it is needed.

The pastor presides at its meetings.

The Puritan Guild is both housekeeper and hostess in the church. In furnishing or refitting it has been of invaluable help to the trustees. It watches over the hospitalities of the parish with such success that the receptions are thronged by those who desire to be friendly. At every meeting missionary work is prepared, distributed, returned, and information from various fields is given.

The Guild welcomes and makes the way easy for those who have a mind to serve. Its treasury is supplied by small weekly gifts.

The Helping Hand devotes itself to the welfare of poor and deserving women. At the weekly meeting after devotional services, these groups of women are taught how to sew, to be tidy, to be thrifty, to buy, to cook, to keep well, to respect themselves, and to know Him who both fed the multitude and also led them into the Kingdom of Heaven.

The time spent by these women in sewing is paid for in garments or in provisions. If they are sick they are cared for. In summer they are sent into the country. At Thanksgiving an abundant dinner is given them to be used at home. In the holidays they dine together in the chapel. In many ways they are made to feel the touch of that divine nature, that kindness which makes the whole world akin.

Envelopes for regular assistance to this noble charity are supplied to those who desire them. Thank-offerings and memorial gifts help on the work. Yet opportunities for a wise use of far greater resources than are now within reach are constantly in view. "The poor ye have always with you."

The Young People's Association keeps informed of the work of the church by written reports, which are read at each meeting. One committee attends to the prayer meeting. Another looks after new members. A third provides the flowers which lend their graceful lesson to the Sabbath service, and then are distributed among the sick in the evening. This committee also provides for the decorations of Easter and Christmas. A fourth committee reports the work of the mission-

ary branch, a devoted company of young ladies who give one afternoon in each week to a careful study of missionary fields, with practical labor and offerings —" full of good works and alms-deeds." The widespread interest and pleasure manifest in this gathering shows how an intelligent, quiet, and earnest devotion

is appreciated. No work could be at once more useful or promising. The privilege of membership is free to all young ladies. A fifth committee makes record of the Puritan Chorus, which does thorough work, led and inspired by the musical director of the church. The Chorus is of great value both to those who enjoy its instruction and to those whom it leads in the worship of festival days. It has greatly endeared itself to all the parish.

The Comfort and Charity Club is composed of girls who sew and plan and become acquainted with the best ways of doing good, and of boys who turn out carpenters' work and learn the art of wood carving. Their special aim is the care of needy children at home and abroad. They are constantly on foot among hospitals, mission-schools, and homes for the destitute. The club is very prosperous. It has earned several hundred dollars this year. It is distinguished by having always a balance in the treasury.

The Little Puritans meet every week with the utmost regularity and devotion to business. Their work is among the nurseries of the City Missions.

These societies, composed of nearly three hundred members, form a system by which every good impulse commencing in childhood is trained into steady and thoughtful habits of Christian labor. All are made to enjoy the special work committed to them, and this spirit is carried on into the next society to which new experiences and duties may lead. Meanwhile, as they go "from strength to strength," they are kept near the church.

It is earnestly desired that the active sympathy of the entire church may insure the continued activity and growth of these societies. They will be of the greatest value to every one so long as this interest "is not strained," but comes graciously from the life of a public sentiment "twice blessed. It blesseth him that gives and him that takes."

From a social point of view it would seem that the most permanent and enjoyable friendships have taken root in a common labor for Christ. In the days of trial such fellowship has been a source of inexhaustible strength and comfort. It is hoped that in all coming church life pleasure in every form will be, not the motive, but the result of devotion to Christ and his brethren.

APPOINTMENTS.

Morning worship is held at 11 A. M. throughout the year.

The time of evening worship is 7.30 P. M. during the winter, and 7.45 during the summer.

Sabbath-school meets at 3 P. M. in both Chapel and Church.

Preparatory Lecture occurs on Wednesday evening preceding Communion.

The Sacrament of the Lord's Supper is administered on the first Sabbath mornings in February, April, June, October, and December, at the close of the regular service.

A Devotional Service is held every Wednesday evening at 8 o'clock.

The Young People's Service of Praise occurs a half-hour before Sabbath evening worship. Also on Saturday evening before Communion.

The Session meets on Tuesday evening preceding the Communion, at the house of the pastor. It holds frequent consultations, as circumstances may direct. Letters to the Church may be given to the pastor at any time. The only formality of receiving letters is the reading of names at the Communion. Letters of Dismission are granted by the Session at their regular meeting.

It is to be desired, in the interest of order and good fellowship, that the custom of taking letters to other Churches on removal and bringing letters from other Churches to this Church, even though the time of new residence be uncertain, should be observed. No influence can safely be overlooked which concerns the spirit of our work and worship.

The time for the Baptism of Children is at the opening of the morning service on the Sabbath following Communion. It may, however, take place at other times as circumstances determine.

"Although it is proper that Baptism be administered in the presence of the Congregation, yet there may be cases when it will be expedient to administer this ordinance in private houses; of which the minister is to be the judge." Directory for Worship, ch. vii., § v.

The Puritan Guild meets on the first Wednesday afternoon of each month, at 3 o'clock, in the Chapel.

The Helping Hand receives its friends on Thursday afternoon at 3 o'clock, in Temperance Hall, Lexington Avenue, near 125th street.

The Young People's Association meets on the third Thursday evening of each month in the Chapel.

The Missionary Branch holds a weekly session on Monday afternoon, at 50 West 130th Street.

The Puritan Chorus rehearsals follow the Wednesday evening service.

The girls of the Comfort and Charity Club may be found at 29 West 130th Street, at 4 o'clock on Friday afternoon. The boys meet at the same place Saturday morning at 8.30, and Saturday evening at 7 o'clock.

The Little Puritans meet at 50 West 130th Street on Tuesday at half-past three o'clock.

Public Offerings are infrequent. On the second Sabbath of the month a General Offering is received, which is divided among the Home and Foreign Missionary, Educational, Freedmen, and other Boards according to the direction of the General Assembly. In this way greater regularity in giving is secured, and the offertory becomes an act of worship rather than an impulse.

At the Lord's Table an Offering is received for the poor of the Church. This has always been abundant.

In order to provide for the constant wants of the building, and still more in the interests of that graceful and indispensable hospitality of free pews, a weekly giving by envelopes is commended. There are many who love to give more than their pews represent, in order to "bear one another's burdens, and so fulfill the law of Christ." To others it may be the only way of contributing to the support of the Church. To the children it becomes the first step of an interest which will at length bring them to the offering of themselves in consecration to Him who reminds us, "Freely ye have received, freely give."

As the amount contributed (week by week through envelopes) is known only to the treasurer of this fund, no form of benevolence is more full of a spirit dear to Him of whom the Lord says, "Thy father which seeth in secret, himself shall reward thee openly." That the blessing may be complete, every one, but most of all the children, need to make these "alms in secret" with self-denial. The apostle has given order, "Concerning the collection. . . . upon the

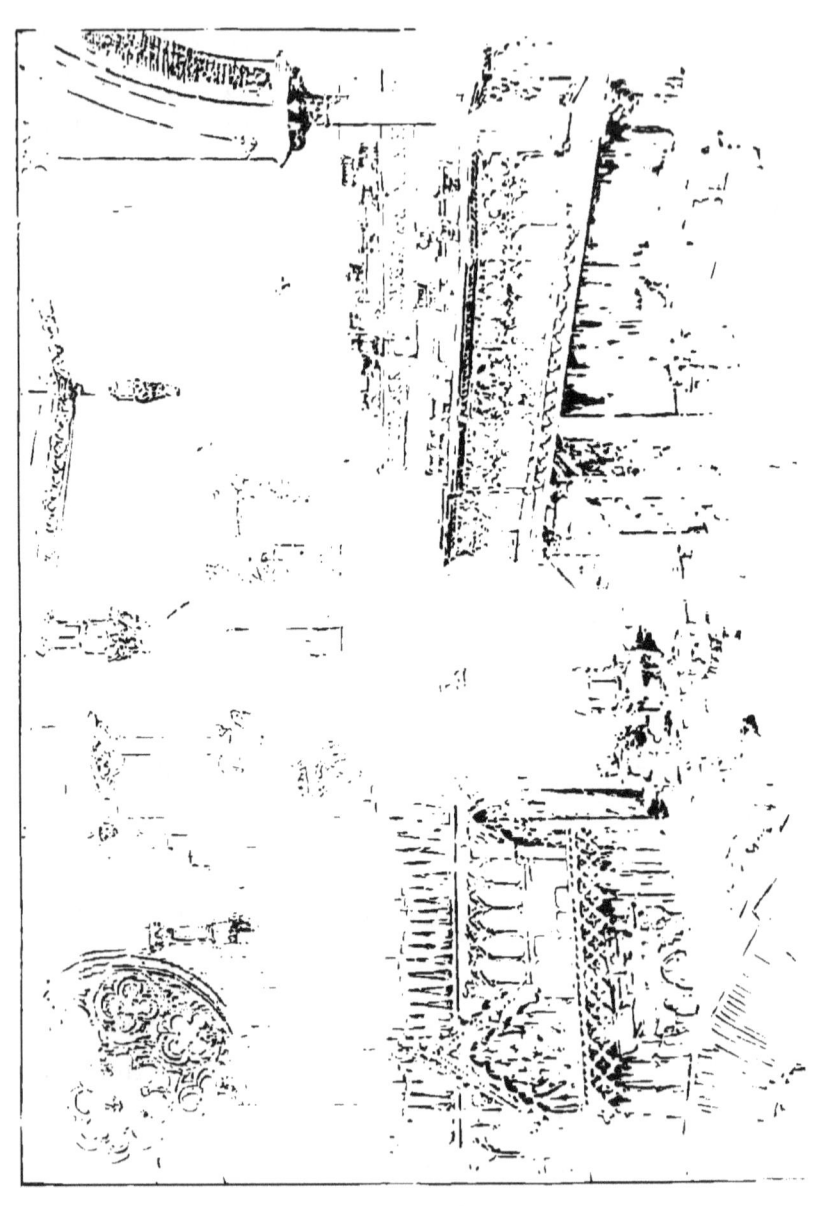

THE NEW YORK
PUBLIC LIBRARY

ASTOR, LENOX
TILDEN FOUNDATIONS

first day of the week let every one of you lay by him in store as God hath prospered him."

The Annual Parish Meeting is held in November.

The Annual Meeting of the Church is held in February.

In some of these lines every one may find rich reward in the use of his peculiar gifts. Let no one forget that in a kind manner, a steady attendance, and earnest purpose he may bring far more prosperity to the Church than money can represent. The kingdom of Christ comes not by many wise, or great, or distinguished services. "Ye see your calling, brethren." "Of him are ye in Christ Jesus, who of God is made unto us wisdom." If any man lack wisdom, let him ask of God, who giveth freely; and receiving, let him communicate unto others.

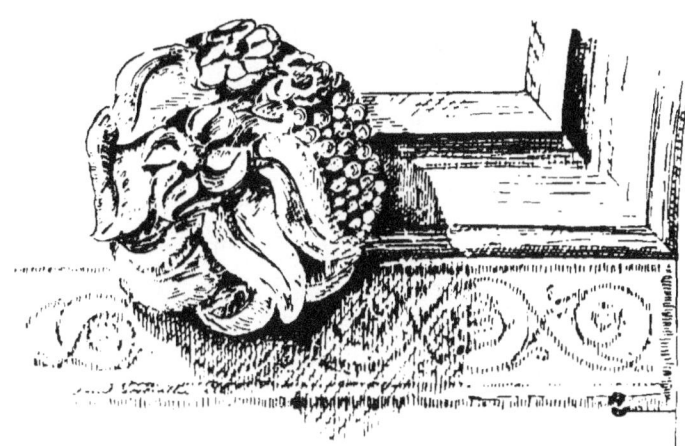

Carved Boss or Hood Moulding
West Transept Window

Membership.

Blessed be God, who hath set up so many clear lamps in his church: and blessed be the memory of those, his faithful servants, who have left their lives and have willingly wasted themselves into these enduring monuments to give light to others.

Bishop Hall.

Of Zion it shall be said, This and that man was born in her: and the Highest himself shall establish her. The Lord shall count, when he writeth up the people, that this man was born there.

Psalm LXXXVII.

MEMBERS are received into the Church by the Session. This usually occurs after personal conference with the Session. But the Session may also, for special reasons, receive those who have seen only the pastor. Those who come for the first time to the Communion are at the Lord's Table informally welcomed by the pastor. The Sacrament of the Lord's Supper is not infrequently administered to the sick in their own home.

The condition of membership is not the same for officers and other communicants. The former are expected to have a more formal outline of belief. The latter, among whom many children are expected to appear, have only to give evidence of trust in Christ as their Divine Saviour. All may come to the Communion who endeavor to obey these commands, " Follow me," " Do this in remembrance of me."

Attention is especially called to the Directory of Worship in the Presbyterian Book of Discipline, Chap. IX., Sec. 1:

"Children, born within the pale of the visible Church, and dedicated to God in baptism, are under the inspection and government of the Church; and are to be taught to read and repeat the Catechism, the Apostle's Creed, and the Lord's Prayer. They are to be taught to pray, to abhor sin, to fear God, and to obey the Lord Jesus Christ. And when they come to years of discretion, if they be free from scandal, appear sober and steady, and to have sufficient knowledge to discern the Lord's body, they ought to be informed it is their duty and their privilege to come to the Lord's Supper."

What the Session understands by the expression "knowledge to discern the Lord's body," is such a view of Christ as may lead them to say, " He loved me and gave himself for me." Then, as daily bread makes them strong, so the word and life of Christ continually received, "in an honest and good heart," will " bring forth fruit with patience."

In their coming and remaining, in worship and service, it is expected that every line of life may meet in one thought, Jesus Christ the Saviour of men.

ORIGINAL MEMBERS.

Abbreviations.— D, Dismissed; * Deceased.

Angell, Carrie E.	
Anner, Peter A.	* 1875
Anner, Margaret	
Anner, Mary Augusta	* 1884
Anner, William S.	* 1873
Anner, Katherine F.	* 1880
Bos, Josephine	* 1888
Brewster, John H.	D 1877
Burnett, William	D 1882
Carman, William S	D 1876
Carman, Sarah A.	D 1876
Carman, Maria A	D 1876
Cooper, Sarah E.	
Cooper, Frank A.	* 1876
Dimon, David F.	D 1879
Dudley, Joseph A	* 1883
Dudley, Eliza H	* 1879
Dye, Larue C.	* 1877
Dye, Margaret H	
Earle, Fanny E.	D 1880
Gardner, George H.	
Gardner, Elizabeth E.	
Hamilton, Martha	
Hawes, Euphenia A.	D 1878
Jenkins, Annetta	D 1884
Jenkins, Fannie	D 1884
Kline, George P	* 1878
Kline, Jane	
Leggett, Edward H.	
Leggett, William	D 1876

MAVER, GEORGE. ..	
MILLER, SILAS W.	D 1878
MILLER, CHARLOTTE S.	D 1878
MILLS, ELIZA FREEBORN.......	
MOORE, ELIZABETH C.	
MOORE, SUSAN A.	
MOORE, ELLEN	
MOORE, LOUISA	
OAKLEY, CLARENCE E.	D 1875
OAKLEY, ANNA L......	D 1875
OAKLEY, KATE A. ....:	* 1873
PURCELL, MARTHA	* 1886
PURCELL, HANNAH	
PURCELL, JANE...............	
RANDALL, S. AUGUSTA......	D 1875
RAWSON, MATTIE H.......	

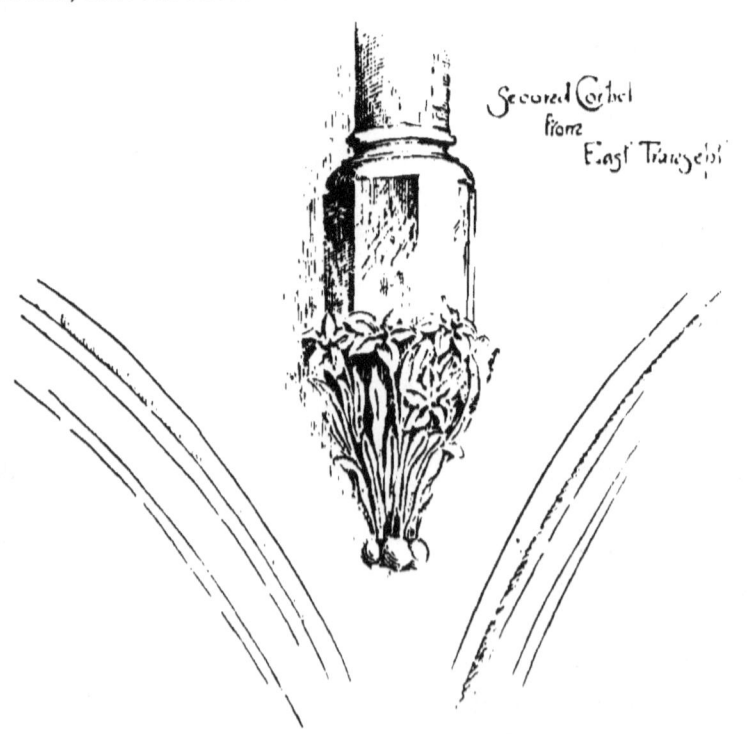

Secured Corbel from East Transept

MEMBERS RECEIVED AND REMOVED.

L, Received by Letter; S, Received by Session; D, Dismissed; * Deceased.

ABBOTT, JOSEPHINE	L 1873	D 1875
ATWATER, WILLIAM	L 1874	* 1882
ATWATER, ELIZABETH H. .	L 1874	* 1881
ALDEN, HELEN W.	S 1881	D 1887
BAIRD, CAROLINE E...................	L 1876	D 1883
BALDWIN, LUCIE E.	L 1884	D 1887
BANKS, DAVID...........	L 1879	D 1887
BANKS, FRANCES L.	L 1879	D 1887
BANKS, SHEPARD	S 1876	D 1887
BARBOUR, W. H.	L 1873	D 1887
BARBOUR, R. G. .	L 1873	D 1887
BAYNE, HENRY....	S 1872	* 1888
BEACH, ARTHUR..........	L 1885	D 1887
BEDFORD, WENDOVER P.......	L 1878	D 1884
BEDFORD, CORNELIA V. O.......	L 1878	D 1884
BEDFORD, CORNELIA C..........	L 1878	D 1884
BELL, CHARLES........	L 1884	D 1885
BELL, ANGELINE....	L 1884	D 1885
BELL, HARRIET N........................	L 1884	D 1885
BELL, GRACE H.......	L 1884	D 1885
BELL, STELLA A........... ...	L 1884	D 1885
BRONSON, HENRY T.	L 1881	D 1883
BRONSON, ELLEN P.	L 1881	D 1883
BUCHAN, JAMES	L 1881	* 1887
BUXTON, CHARLES F.	L 1879	D 1885
BUXTON, SARAH RICHARD	L 1879	D 1885
BUXTON, CHARLOTTE F...........	S 1883	D 1885

MEMBERSHIP

CAMPBELL, MARIE.. ...	L 1874	D 1882
CAMP, ANNA JOSEPHINE...	L 1872	D 1880
CARMAN, WILLIAM BANKS	S 1873	D 1876
CARR, D. C......	L 1877	D 1883
CASTLE, SAMUEL A.....	L 1883	* 1887
CHAPIN, GARDENER S	L 1877	D 1879
CHAPIN, ELIZABETH W	L 1877	D 1879
CHAPIN, ANNIE L.......	L 1877	D 1879
CHAPIN, FRANK H.......	L 1877	D 1879
CHAPIN, CHARLOTTE E.	S 1887	D 1879
CHAPIN, MAGGIE........	L 1877	D 1879
CLARK, SAMUEL J............	L 1873	D 1885
CLARK, SARAH J............	L 1873	D 1885
CONGER, MRS. W. E. M	L 1886	D 1887
CONGER, SADIE E............	L 1886	D 1887
COOK, ELIZA...........................	S 1880	* 1881
COOPER, CORNELIA	S 1873	D 1888
CRAMER, URSULA S......	S 1880	* 1881
CROSBY, WILLIAM B..............	L 1882	D 1886
DALY, CHARITY.............	L 1885	* 1887
DENNIS, HOLMES V. M	S 1876	D 1878
DENNIS, MRS. H. V..	S 1876	D 1878
DODD, S. C. T.....	L 1882	D 1885
DODD, SARAH B	L 1882	D 1885
DODD, MARY E...	L 1882	D 1885
DODD, FRED G......	S 1883	D 1885
DUDLEY, WILLIAM B	S 1873	D 1887
DUNHAM, MARY H...	L 1874	* 1879
DUNNE, ANNIE C..	S 1875	D 1886
DUNNING, ELIZABETH	L 1874	D 1886
DUSENBURY, BESSIE......	S 1885	D 1887
EARLE, MARGARET.	S 1874	D 1880

THE CHURCH OF THE PURITANS

Easton, Robert Janes...	s 1886	d 1887
Elton, C. Clark	s 1879	d 1880
Elwell, Cornelius L.	l 1887	* 1887
Felter, L.	l 1884	d 1887
Ferris, Frank A.	l 1879	d 1886
Ferris, Mary A.	l 1879	d 1886
Ferris, Helen	s 1881	d 1886
Ferris, Jennie	s 1881	d 1886
Ferris, Walter R.	s 1882	d 1886
Ferris, Belle	s 1882	d 1886
Ferris, Susan	l 1877	* 1879
Fisk, Harvey Edward	l 1879	d 1886
Fisk, Mary L.	l 1879	d 1886
Fisk, Charles J.	l 1880	d 1887
Fisk, Lillie R.	l 1880	d 1887
Gilson, Emma	l 1877	d 1888
Gilson, Elizabeth F.	s 1878	d 1888
Gilson, Walter	s 1883	d 1888
Gilson, William H.	s 1883	d 1888
Goodale, Samuel B.	l 1874	d 1881
Goodale, Josephine C.	l 1874	d 1881
Grant, Jennie Porter	l 1887	d 1888
Grey, Jane F.	s 1878	* 1879
Griffiths, Kate	l 1878	d 1882
Griffiths, Margaret	l 1873	d 1875
Hallock, Edward H.	l 1873	d 1877
Hallock, Mary E.	l 1873	d 1877
Hallock, Edgar Sherwood	s 1875	d 1877
Hallock, Anna Louisa	s 1875	d 1877
Hance, Isaac A.	l 1874	d 1877
Hance, Louisa A.	l 1874	d 1877

MEMBERSHIP

HAND, EUGENE S	L 1880	D 1882
HAND, MARY......	L 1880	D 1882
HARRIS, M. EDWARD	S 1886	* 1886
HASTINGS, GEORGE S..	L 1877	D 1880
HASTINGS, HARRIET M	L 1877	D 1880
HILL, GEORGE......	L 1874	* 1879
HOLT, JOSEPH S..	L 1875	D 1885
HOLT, LUCY A......	L 1875	D 1885
JACKSON, HENRY M	L 1873	D 1883
JACKSON, INEZ B ..	S 1873	* 1879
JARDINE, EDWARD......	L 1873	D 1875
JARVIS, OLIVER A......	L 1881	* 1885
JOHNSON, HENRIETTA W	L 1873	D 1884
JOHNSON, CHARLES O	L 1883	D 1887
JOHNSON, S. L..	L 1883	D 1887
KENNEDY, WILLIAM.....	L 1876	* 1877
KETCHUM, ALEXANDER P.	L 1879	D 1886
KETCHUM, CLARA D..	L 1879	D 1886
KETCHUM, LILLIAN D	S 1885	D 1886
KILPATRICK, SAMUEL..	L 1883	D 1885
KILPATRICK, BETTY J....	L 1883	D 1885
KILPATRICK, HELEN.......	L 1883	D 1885
KILPATRICK, MARY F.	L 1883	D 1885
LATHROP, ASA S........	L 1878	* 1880
LESTRADE, MARY C....	L 1874	D 1886
LESTRADE, FRANCIS W	L 1874	D 1886
LEWIS, ELIZABETH M.	L 1877	D 1880
LYON, WILLIAM S.......	L 1872	D 1885
LYTTLE, EUGENE D.....	L 1882	D 1884
MANN, EDWARD C	L 1875	D 1879

Manson, Clara Houghton........	L 1885	* 1887
Marvin, Frederick R..............	L 1875	D 1887
Marvin, Persis A...	S 1877	D 1881
Marvin, Samuel W	L 1879	D 1887
Marvin, Susan D..................	L 1879	D 1887
Maxwell, Alexander............	L 1872	* 1880
Maxwell, Charles M.........	S 1872	D 1876
McElhenney, Jane W........	L 1883	D 1885
McElhenney, Sarah A..	L 1883	D 1885
McElhenney, Rebecca....	L 1883	D 1885
McElhenney, Margaret..	L 1883	D 1885
McElhenney, Agnes........	L 1883	D 1885
Merwin, Berkeley R......	L 1882	D 1887
Merwin, Florence R	L 1882	D 1887
Mott, Sarah M...........	L 1881	D 1887
Oakley, Anna ...	L 1872	D 1872
Oakley, Ruth...	L 1872	D 1874
Olliffe, William M	S 1885	* 1885
Palmer, William K.	L 1876	D 1881
Paret, Esther Elizabeth.	L 1879	D 1888
Paret, Anna Pamly....................	S 1882	D 1888
Paret, Caroline E..........	S 1882	D 1888
Paret, Annie Elizabeth...	L 1882	D 1888
Patters, Emily.......	S 1874	* 1886
Patterson, Sarah.......	L 1876	* 1877
Patterson, George T., Jr.	L 1876	D 1887
Patterson, Emma L..............	L 1876	D 1887
Patterson, Ruby...............	S 1885	D 1887
Peet, Louisa P........................	L 1877	D 1883
Pickford, Salina...........	S 1873	* 1880
Pirnie, Ann..	L 1876	* 1887
Poillon, Mary G	L 1882	D 1883

MEMBERSHIP

POILLON, MARY E...	L 1882	D 1883
POILLON, IDA C...............	L 1882	D 1883
PROUDFOOT, AUGUSTA...................	S 1887	* 1887
RENWICK, WILLIAM C..............	L 1873	D 1884
RENWICK, HARRIET McD................	L 1873	* 1877
RICHARDS, SARAH M....................	L 1879	* 1882
ROAHR, CECILIA.......	L 1875	D 1884
ROAHR, BELLA......	S 1880	D 1884
ROAHR, MINNIE..............	S 1880	D 1884
ROBERTS, ROBERT M...................	S 1878	* 1880
ROBERTS, CAROLINE J..............	S 1875	* 1875
ROBERTS, HATTIE W............	L 1878	D 1887
ROBERTS, ELLA W........	S 1878	D 1887
ROSS, SAMUEL P..................	L 1880	* 1887
ROSS, LUTHEREA......................	L 1880	D 1883
RUSH, CORDELIA............	L 1877	D 1885
RUSH, ANNA L.............	L 1877	D 1887
SAYRE, SARAH LUCRETIA.....	L 1879	* 1880
SCHENCK, MINNIE F.................	L 1880	* 1885
SAXE, MARION..........................	S 1882	D 1886
SEARS, GERTRUDE C................	S 1878	D 1884
SHEKELTON, WILLIAM N	L 1884	* 1886
SHEPARD, SARAH R......................	L 1875	* 1878
SMITH, TRYPHENIA N................	L 1879	* 1883
SMITH, WESLEY................	L 1887	D 1888
SMITH, MRS. WESLEY.....................	L 1887	D 1888
SMITH, ABEL H.....................	L 1873	D 1881
SMITH, ELIZABETH.................	L 1873	D 1881
SOLOMON, ELIZA ROGERS...........	L 1880	D 1884
SOLOMON, ELLA LOUISA..............	L 1880	D 1884
SOLOMON, FLORENCE HARVEY.....	L 1880	D 1884
SPRAGUE, SUSAN A....................	L 1874	D 1876

STANTON, KATE C.	L 1878	* 1881
STEVENS, JANE	L 1875	D 1878
STEVENS, JENNIE	L 1875	D 1878
STEVENS, GEORGE ALEXANDER	L 1875	D 1878
ST. JOHN, PHEBE	L 1875	* 1877
STORRS, AARON P	L 1875	D 1876
STORRS, LOUISA P.	L 1875	D 1876
STRAHAN, AGNES	L 1880	* 1885
STREETER, R. M.	L 1873	D 1876
STREETER, HATTIE D.	L 1873	D 1876
STRONG, HENRY T.	L 1873	* 1876
STRONG, MARY C.	L 1873	D 1884
TAYLOR, GRACE A.	L 1877	D 1881
TREFFENBERG, EMILY C.	S 1885	D 1887
TREFFENBERG, EMILY N	S 1885	D 1887
TREFFENBERG, LOUISA W.	S 1885	D 1887
TREHARNE, CAROLINE	L 1876	D 1880
TRUAX, NANCY STONE	L 1874	* 1886
TRUAX, JOHN G.	L 1877	D 1885
TURNER, MRS. J.	L 1886	* 1887
VANCOTT, THEODORE S.	S 1876	D 1882
VANCOTT, ROSELLE C.	S 1877	D 1881
VAN DOREN, HELEN WYNKOOP	L 1885	D 1888
WARREN, REV. J. C.	L 1875	* 1883
WARREN, SARAH S	L 1876	D 1879
WATERBURY, HARRIET	L 1884	* 1888
WHITE, CHARLES B.	L 1880	D 1884
WHITE, MRS. CHARLES B	S 1880	D 1884
WILLIS, HARRIET	L 1878	* 1887
WOOD, EDWARD A.	L 1886	D 1887
WOOD, NANCY E. C.	L 1886	D 1887

WOODWARD, JOHN W.	L 1881	D 1886
WOODWARD, MARY T.	L 1881	D 1886
WRIGHT, MARGARET S.	S 1880	D 1887

PRESENT MEMBERS.

February, 1889.

L, Received by Letter; S, Received by Session.

ALLING, EMMA H.	L 1888
ANDERSON, ANNIE	L 1875
ANDERSON, FANNIE R	S 1876
ANDERSON, HELEN W.	S 1876
ANDERSON, LYDIA	L 1875
ANDERSON, ELIZABETH	L 1888
ANDERSON, ADA ISABEL	L 1888
ANDERSON, KATE M.	L 1888
ANDERSON, LILLIAN MOFFAT.	L 1888
ANGELL, CARRIE E.	L 1872
ANNER, JAMES H.	S 1877
ANNER, ALICE	S 1877
ANNER, MARGARET	L 1872
ATWATER, ELIZABETH	L 1874
ATWATER, LAURA A.	S 1875
ATWATER, WILLIAM E.	S 1875
ACTON, JOHN WHITTAKER	L 1889
ACTON, CARRIE H.	L 1889
BAILEY, DANIEL DREW	S 1887
BAILEY, ELLA	S 1882
BAILEY, FLORENCE	S 1887
BAKER, BOMAN C.	L 1888
BAKER, EDWIN M.	L 1888

Baldwin, Truman H............................	L 1884
Baldwin, Caroline H......................	L 1884
Baldwin, Lesa L. Sage......................	L 1884
Banning, Herbert A........................	L 1883
Banning, Viola H. S........................	S 1883
Barnes, Sarah C.............................	L 1887
Barrett, Angeline M......................	L 1887
Barrett, Blanche Addie	S 1887
Barrett, Frank B...........................	S 1888
Bayne, Jane D................................	S 1881
Beach, Joshua M............................	L 1880
Beach, Carrie K.............................	L 1880
Beach, Grace B..............................	L 1880
Beach, Elizabeth S.........................	L 1880
Beach, Sarah E...............................	L 1880
Beach, Maurice J...........................	S 1880
Beals, James Henry, Jr...................	S 1886
Beals, Mary Francis........................	S 1886
Beals, Annie Read..........................	S 1886
Black, A. Stewart..........................	L 1880
Black, Ann E.................................	L 1880
Black, Annie Acherson....................	S 1882
Black, Margaret.............................	L 1880
Black, Reed Fulton.........................	S 1882
Black, Wallace...............................	L 1880
Blanchard, Addie Lefferts...............	L 1882
Blaisdell, James H.........................	L 1872
Blaisdell, Helen M.........................	L 1872
Bogart, James................................	L 1883
Bogart, Mary.................................	L 1883
Bos, John......................................	L 1872
Boyce, Harriet...............................	L 1883
Brockway, William Joseph...............	L 1889
Brockway, Addie B.........................	L 1888

BROWN, ALEXANDER...	S 1881
BUCHAN, RACHEL.....	L 1881
BUCHAN, SARAH	L 1881
BUCHAN, ANNIE......	L 1881
BUCHAN, DAISY.................	S 1889
BURDELL, EMELINE L............	L 1883
BURKE, WILLIAM E.............	S 1876
BURKE, AMELIA AUGUSTA...........	L 1876
CABLE, CORNELIA HOWLAND	L 1873
CAMPS, FRANCIS	L 1872
CARSS, JOHN.....	L 1883
CARSS, MARIAN	L 1883
CARSS, JOHN B	L 1883
CARSS, MARY C..................	L 1883
CARSS, HARRIET......	S 1886
CARSS, ELIZABETH.............	S 1887
CARINGTON, ELIZA M..........	L 1885
CASTLE, MARY A	L 1883
CLARK, ELTON C.	S 1884
CLARK, HARRIE E..	L 1885
CLARK, JULIA S.......	L 1884
CLARK, STEPHEN S..........	L 1884
CLARK, SUSAN LORD..............	L 1872
CLARK, SUSAN GRAFTON...........	L 1872
CLARK, MAUD MARY...........	L 1885
CLARK, MARY........	S 1888
COLWELL, W. H...........	L 1885
COLWELL, CARRIE I.....	L 1885
COOK, JOHN C............................	L 1880
COOK, JENNIE.......................	S 1881
COOK, MABEL..........	S 1888
COOPER, SARAH E................	L 1872
COOPER, EDGAR H..........	S 1880

Cooper, Amy L.	s 1873
Cox, Emma F.	L 1882
Cox, Elizabeth R.	L 1882
Cox, Mary A.	L 1882
Cummins, Henry I.	L 1877
Cummins, Julia A.	L 1877
Currier, James W.	L 1877
Currier, Addie L.	s 1882
Currier, Mabel	s 1875
Cutler, Josephine M.	L 1882
Daeniker, Henry H.	L 1888
Daeniker, Mary T.	L 1888
Daeniker, E.	s 1887
Daeniker, Maude Goutard	s 1887
Daly, Charles	L 1885
Daly, Ella B.	L 1885
Davis, Martha W.	L 1873
Dawson, Adelaide	s 1876
Dayton, Charles W	s 1888
Depew, Robert A.	L 1877
Dickinson, Frederic E.	L 1885
Dickinson, Julia R.	L 1885
Donald, James	L 1883
Donald, Mary	L 1883
Dow, Joseph E.	s 1886
Dow, Annie E.	s 1879
Dow, Mamie E.	s 1883
Dow, Lotta	s 1883
Dow, Nannie A.	s 1887
Dunbar, James R.	s 1886
Dwight, John	L 1879
Dwight, Mary E.	L 1879
Dwight, Marion	L 1879

MEMBERSHIP

Dye, Margaret H.................................... L 1872
Dye, Martha Rice .... S 1873
Dyer, Herbert S..................................... S 1881
Dyer, Lizzie M..................................... S 1881

Easton, Robert T. B............................... L 1884
Easton, L. Josephine.............................. L 1884
Easton, Alice...................................... S 1887
Elder, Robert D.................................... L 1883
Elder, Mary E...................................... L 1883
Elwell, L. D....................................... L 1887
Ely, Philo S....................................... L 1886
Ely, Esther V. O................................... L 1886
Erdenbracker, Adelaide............................. L 1882
Erwin, Frank A..................................... L 1887
Erwin, Ella Reaumount.............................. L 1887
Evans, Edward C.................................... L 1887
Evans, Esther Elizabeth............................ S 1887
Euen, Mary E....................................... L 1883
Euen, Louise Chapin................................ S 1883

Farr, Mary C....................................... L 1886
Finney, Helen...................................... S 1888
Folsom, Carrie .... L 1880
Folsom, Blanche S.................................. S 1879
Foote, Howard W.................................... L 1880
Foote, Josephine................................... S 1880
Fox, Ewing... L 1873
Fox, Amelia.. L 1873
Freeborn, Edith R.................................. S 1873

Gardner, George H.................................. L 1872
Gardner, Elizabeth E............................... L 1872
Gardner, Euretta Elizabeth......................... S 1880

GARDNER, MARY C.	L 1881
GARDNER, FRANK S.	L 1884
GARDNER, FANNY E.	L 1881
GARDNER, MRS. FRANK S.	L 1881
GARDNER, ANNIE A.	L 1881
GARDENER, ELLA	L 1881
GEDNEY, DELIA M.	L 1879
GEDNEY, REBECCA	L 1887
GILBERT, HORATIO G.	L 1887
GILBERT, ALICE MAUD	L 1886
GILBERT, SUSAN	L 1888
GILBERT, SUSAN STEVENS	L 1887
GILBERT, LOUISE TAYLOR	L 1886
GOODALE, MAUDE M.	S 1874
GRAY, CLOYDON L.	S 1878
HALLOCK, JEANNETTE R.	L 1881
HAMILTON, JOHN ANDREWS	S 1873
HAMILTON, MARTHA	L 1872
HANFORD, WILLIAM H.	S 1888
HANFORD, MRS. WM. H.	S 1888
HARRIS, SARAH M.	L 1885
HEALEY, CLARK	L 1873
HEALEY, HARRIET A.	L 1873
HEBRON, J. M.	L 1889
HEBRON, R. H.	L 1889
HELZLER, CHARLES	S 1875
HILL, KATE M.	L 1873
HILL, EMMA	L 1873
HILL, MAY BELLE	L 1874
HILL, SOPHIA	S 1874
HILL, GEORGE ALBERT	S 1881
HILL, MAY BELLE	S 1883
HINCHMAN, LUCINDA E.	S 1887

MEMBERSHIP

Hinchman, Marion A.. S 1887
Hitchcock, Alice... S 1883
Holbrook, Anna Chalmers... L 1889
Holmes, Hannie L.. L 1879
Horne, Peter... L 1881
Horne, Lucinda M.. L 1881
Hume, Harriet Ely... S 1886
Humphrey, Jane S.. L 1879
Humphrey, Jane.. S 1880

Jarvis, Catherine A... L 1881
Jarvis, Ida May... L 1881
Jones, May Virginia... S 1887
Jones, Alice Byell.. L 1887

Kehler, Harriet A... S 1879
Kelly, Lillie B... L 1888
Kennedy, Margaret J... L 1876
Kennedy, Mary S... L 1876
Kline, Jane... L 1872
Kline, Fannie R... S 1878

Lane, Henry... L 1884
Lane, Sarah T... L 1884
Landers, Katharine.. S 1888
Landers, Mildred Edith.. S 1888
Landis, Alfred S.. L 1887
Landis, Thomas J. T... L 1888
Landis, Lillie M.. L 1888
Lathrop, Caroline S... L 1878
Lathrop, Carrie J... L 1878
Lathrop, James R.. L 1879
Lathrop, Mary E... L 1879
Lay, George C... L 1888

Lay, Sarah Emma	L 1888
Lefferts, Lewis	L 1882
Lefferts, Phœbe	L 1882
Lefferts, Flora	L 1882
Lefferts, Annie B	S 1884
Lefferts, Lillie	S 1885
Leggett, Edward H	L 1872
Leonard, Austin L	L 1889
Leonard, Maria E	L 1889
Leonard, Alice E	L 1889
Leonard, Mabel C	L 1889
L'Esperance, David Andrew	S 1888
L'Esperance, Margaret L	L 1884
Lestrade, Annie L	S 1875
Lestrade, James W	L 1874
Lima, Charles C	L 1883
Lima, Julia E	L 1883
Lima, Alice M	L 1883
Longstreet, Sarah E	L 1878
Lucas, Edward F	L 1883
Lucas, Martha T. N	L 1883
Mackenzie, John	L 1872
Mann, Reuben S	L 1880
Mann, Mrs. Reuben S	L 1880
Mann, Lewis Francis	S 1883
Mann, Addie B	S 1883
Manning, C. C	L 1886
Manning, Isabella	L 1886
Maring, Etta	L 1889
Maring, Gertrude Livingstone	L 1889
Mattison, William R	L 1889
Mattison, Fannie L	L 1889
Mattison, Helen V	L 1889

MEMBERSHIP 81

Maver, George	L	1872
Martyn, Stella	S	1873
Maxwell, Sarah R	L	1872
Maxwell, Florence A	L	1872
McGuffog, Grace	L	1887
McKechnie, Elizabeth	L	1875
McKechnie, Elizabeth A	L	1885
McKechnie, Margaret J	L	1875
McKenzie, Sadie	S	1882
McKenzie, Emma	S	1875
Meade, Mary	S	1886
Meade, Jennie Benton	S	1886
Merritt, Edward	S	1873
Merritt, Annie	S	1873
Merritt, Peter S	S	1888
Merritt, Helen Rebecca	S	1880
Metzler, Charles	S	1882
Mills, Isaac	S	1872
Mills, Eliza Freeborn	L	1872
Mills, Benjamin F	S	1885
Mills, Wm. Judson Blydenburg	S	1887
Meigs, Jane T	L	1876
Meigs, Walter	S	1877
Moore, Anna M	L	1889
Moland, Isaac B	L	1889
Moland, Abby	S	1889
Moore, Elizabeth C	L	1872
Moore, Susan A	L	1872
Moore, Ellen	L	1872
Moore, Louisa	L	1872
Morrison, Mary Louise	S	1874
Morse, Rosina S	L	1878
Mott, J. Varnum	L	1881
Mott, Mrs. J. L	S	1885

82   THE CHURCH OF THE PURITANS

Montague, George E.	L	1888
Mulford, George T.	L	1889
Mulford, Martha W.	L	1889
Nicholson, George B.	L	1884
Nicholson, Helen	L	1884
Nicholson, Jessie	L	1884
Nicholson, Rebecca M	L	1884
Nicholson, Mary Helen	S	1887
Nicholson, Charles M.	S	1888
Niebuhr, Helen L.	S	1888
Northrop, A.	L	1882
Northrop, Florence	L	1882
Oliffe, Marie M.	S	1885
Paine, William H	L	1886
Paine, Catherine G	L	1886
Paine, Kathreen L	L	1886
Paret, Henry	S	1882
Paret, Elizabeth	S	1879
Paret, Charlotte E	S	1879
Parsons, Theron E	L	1887
Parsons, Sarah D	L	1887
Parsons, Helen A	L	1887
Paton, T. C. M.	L	1878
Paton, James Morton	L	1878
Paton, Margaret L	L	1878
Paton, Lucy Allen	L	1878
Patterson, Thomas C.	L	1876
Patterson, Clara	L	1876
Patterson, Helen B	S	1882
Patterson, Ella	L	1875
Platt, James D.	L	1878

MEMBERSHIP 83

PLATT, M. AUGUSTA	L	1878
PLATT, DWIGHT MORGAN	S	1881
PLATT, CARRIE MAUD	S	1882
PRESSINGER, WHITEFIELD PRICE	S	1887
PRESSINGER, AUSTIN EDMUND	S	1885
PRESSINGER, ARNOTT MELTON	S	1885
PRESSINGER, SALLETTA MARIE	S	1887
PRESSINGER, MARY DAVIS	S	1887
PRICHARD, ANNIE	L	1881
PURCELL, JANE	L	1872
PURCELL, HANNAH	L	1872
QUICK, CHARLOTTE M	L	1880
RANSOM, WILLIAM H	L	1885
RANSOM, MRS. WILLIAM H	L	1885
RANSOM, EDITH	L	1886
RAWSON, MATTIE H	L	1872
REDDY, SARAH LEWIS	L	1887
REDFIELD, HENRY	L	1889
REDFIELD, JULIA M	L	1889
REDFIELD, HARRIET A	L	1889
REDFIELD, ADA M	L	1889
REED, FREDERICK	S	1884
REED, CORNELIA BEARDSLEY	S	1884
REED, MARY CLARK	S	1884
REID, MRS. EDWARD A	L	1883
REID, ARCHIBALD EDWARD	L	1886
REID, ELIZABETH A	L	1883
REID, JENNIE H	L	1883
REID, LILLIE A	L	1883
REID, MRS. JAMES M	L	1883
RENWICK, ELIZA CROSBY	S	1879
RENWICK, ELLEN	S	1873

Rich. Josephine B.	L 1884
Rigney, Thomas	L 1881
Rigney, Caroline M.	L 1881
Rigney, Charles D.	S 1882
Rowe, Amonta T.	L 1879
Rush, Thomas J.	L 1879
Rush, Ella H.	L 1877
Ryan, Flora	S 1876
Schaff, Anselm	L 1875
Schaff, Helen S.	L 1875
Schell, Alice Adeline	S 1888
Schenck, Remson	L 1880
Scholefield, Helen M.	L 1889
Scholefield, Virginia M.	L 1889
Scott, Albert E.	L 1879
Scott, Mrs. Albert E.	L 1879
Sears, Marion J.	S 1878
Sears, Susan A.	L 1879
Shekelton, Catherine Ann	L 1884
Sherlock, May Lillian	S 1884
Shutes, Samuel E.	L 1878
Shutes, Frank A.	L 1879
Shutes, Sarah B.	L 1878
Shutes, Carrie L.	L 1878
Shutes, Elizabeth Weed	S 1885
Shutes, Marianne	S 1882
Simmons, Simeon	L 1885
Simmons, Elizabeth	L 1885
Simmons, Egbert W.	L 1873
Skinner, Sarah	L 1878
Skinner, Annie	L 1878
Skinner, Minnie	S 1879
Skinner, Florence Amelia	S 1882

MEMBERSHIP 85

Slawson, Mary O.	L	1880
Smith, Edward	L	1885
Smith, Mrs. Edward	L	1885
Smith, Blanche	S	1882
Smith, Nettie T.	L	1887
Smith, George Moore	S	1875
Smith, Anna M.	S	1874
Smith, Sarah Agnes	S	1875
Smith, Elliott	S	1887
Smith, Edwin C.	L	1873
Smith, Abel H.	L	1873
Smith, Elizabeth	L	1873
Smith, Angeline	L	1877
Sniffen, Mary F.	L	1886
Spalding, George A.	L	1880
Spalding, Rebecca A.	L	1880
Stanton, Mrs. Samuel B.	L	1878
Stanton, Mary	L	1878
Stevens, Mary E.	L	1885
Stillman, Edwin E.	S	1887
Stillwell, Elizabeth	L	1875
Strahan, James	S	1880
Streeter, Elizabeth Weed	S	1887
Townsend, Lizzie Bentley	S	1885
Trested, Warren C.	S	1879
Truax, Chauncy Schaffer	L	1876
Turner, Frank	S	1886
Turner, Kate	S	1886
Valentine, William	L	1886
Valentine, Mary H.	L	1886
Valentine, Mary Spies	S	1886
Valentine, Frances Amenda	S	1886

Van Doren, Amelia A	L 1885
Van Doren, Augusta Vael	S 1885
Van Dolson, A. V	L 1885
Van Hoesen, Alice M	L 1889
Van Tuyl, Andrew	L 1879
Van Tuyl, Mrs. Andrew	L 1879
Van Tuyl, Mary E	L 1879
Voorhies, Adelaine	L 1872
Walker, Alva S	L 1878
Walker, Grace Emily	S 1879
Walker, Edith May	S 1879
Walker, William Isaac	L 1883
Waller, Fannie M	L 1880
Warren, Nellie M	L 1876
Waterbury, Frederick Prime	S 1887
Waterbury, Mary	L 1883
Wells, Mrs. W. C	L 1886
Wells, Ella L	L 1886
Wendell, David S	L 1876
Wendell, Mary C	L 1876
Wendell, James W. F	S 1879
Wendell, Charles A	S 1881
Wendell, Ida May	S 1887
White, Harriet M	S 1887
Williams, Arthur	L 1881
Williams, Hattie Stone	L 1881
Williams, Mary E	L 1879
Wiswall, William McAlpine	S 1876
Wiswall, Louise B	S 1876
Wood, Thomas H	L 1875
Wood, Elizabeth	L 1875
Wood, Mary W	L 1887
Woodward, Charles H	L 1880

WOODWARD, ELIZABETH H.	L 1880
WOODWARD, ANNA CORA.	L 1880
WOODWARD, COLLIN H.	L 1880
YOUNG, HUGH.	L 1888
YOUNG, ANNIE C.	L 1888
YOUNG, MARY H.	S 1888

For my brethren and companions' sakes, I will now say, Peace be within thee. Because of the house of the Lord our God, I will seek thy good.

PSALM CXXII.

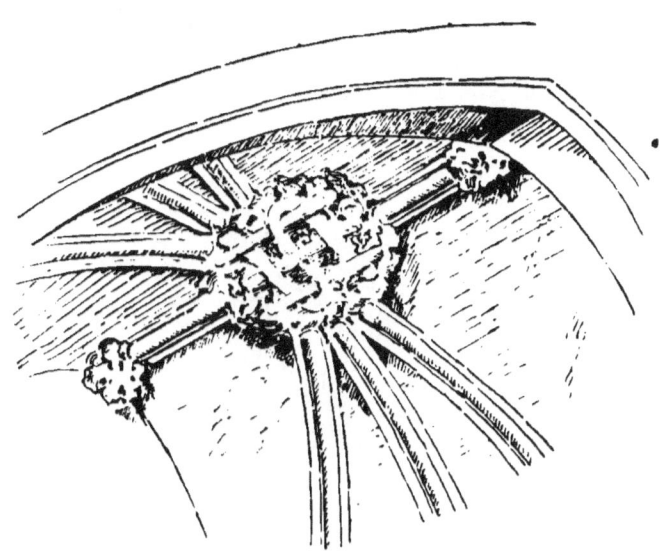

Boss in Chancel

www.ingramcontent.com/pod-product-compliance
Lightning Source LLC
Chambersburg PA
CBHW020158170426
43199CB00010B/1095